The Jimmer Fredette Story

Beyond the Arc

By Kathleen Tracy
and
Jeremy C. Reed

Copyright © 2012 Reed Media Services

Beyond the Arc:
The Jimmer Fredette Story

By Kathleen Tracy and Jeremy C. Reed

Cover photos: David C Harrison
Cover design: Getty Creations

Publisher: Reed Media Services
Website: http://www.reedmedia.net/
September 2012

ISBN: 978-1-937516-02-4

Contents

1	The Best Scorer in the World	1
2	Chip off the Old Block	5
3	Team Sports	17
4	"He's a Freshman!"	21
5	Motivation	25
6	Working Out	31
7	Recruitment	39
8	Senior Season!	45
9	Transition	51
10	Stepping Up	55
11	Legend in the Making	57
12	Amazing	63
13	Drafted	69
14	Lockout	79
15	Sacramento's New King	85

1 The Best Scorer in the World

The Marriott Center Arena in Provo, Utah, was electrified. A sellout crowd of 22,700 stomping and cheering Brigham Young University fans were on their feet as the BYU Cougars basketball team took to the floor for the biggest game of the season. Ranked 7th, they were playing their Mountain West Conference rival on national television, the undefeated San Diego State University Aztecs, ranked 4th in the country. It wasn't often the conference boasted two Top Ten teams. The winner would not only take over the top spot in the Mountain West, but it would also make a strong case for being one of the 64 teams selected for the NCAA tournament. Neither school was accustomed to getting much national attention from the selection committee so the stakes were high for the universities, the teams, and the individual players alike.

Within minutes of the tip off, there was a sense in the partisan crowd that it was going to be a special night for the team and its star point guard Jimmer Fredette and they were not disappointed.

While it may have been a bitterly cold night outside, inside Jimmer was on fire the entire game.

In the first half, Jimmer single-handedly kept the Cougars in the game, scoring the last 15 points for his team. Then in the second half, the Aztecs went as cold as the Utah winter, going nine minutes without scoring a basket and allowing the Cougars to pull away. And when Jimmer sank back to back three-pointers, the Cougar faithful knew the game was theirs and began chanting "You got Jimmmered!"

Jimmer scored 43 points in the Cougars 71-58 victory — the most ever by a BYU player at the Marriott Center — and grabbed four rebounds as well, despite being double-teamed for most of the game. But BYU fans had come to expect heroics from the unassuming player, the leading scorer in the nation who had been on a shooting tear, scoring 40 or more points in three of the Cougars' previous four games. Over the past twelve months he had gone from relative anonymity to a contender for collegiate player of the year.

Even professional players were taking notice. Oklahoma City NBA star Kevin Durant tweeted after the game: "Jimmer Fredette is the best scorer in the world!!"

Already considered by many as the greatest BYU hoops player in the university's history, Jimmer was in the process of creating a legacy as one of the NCAA's all time great basketball stars. In

The Best Scorer in the World

some respects, he was an unlikely star. By basketball standards, he's small, standing just 6'2" and he'll never win a dunking contest. Some say Jimmer's not particularly quick and he'd be banged out of the post, but he's smart, has a wicked crossover dribble, and is a deadeye shooter reminiscent of a young Larry Bird who can make a 30-foot jump shot seem effortless.

While Jimmer's talent can be jaw-dropping, his personal journey from small town boy to national role model is an inspiring story of how family, faith, and fortitude led him to the top of his game.

He was the pop sensation of college basketball — a wunderkind who captured the imaginations of millions and inspired a rap song, "Teach Me How to Jimmer," that turned into a YouTube sensation. He is a role model to millions of young boys and girls who dream of being the best they can be. But to friends and family, he's simply Jimmer, the apple-cheeked all-American boy who happens to be a wizard with a basketball. But none of it came easy; while many people are natural-born athletes, only those willing to work hard and dedicate themselves to a sport will succeed like Jimmer.

2 Chip off the Old Block

James Taft Fredette was born February 25, 1989, in Glens Falls, New York, but from the day he was born, he was known as Jimmer. His mom Kay explains the nickname came about to distinguish him from several other family members named James.

The name actually came from Kay's friend's little brother when she was just a young girl. "I always thought that it was cute and twenty or more years later when I had my last son, I remembered that name because Jimmer looked like a Jimmer, full of energy and character ... I just went with my instincts," Kay said.

Kay admits she became annoyed with teachers who called her son James, because she didn't believe he identified with his birth name. She also felt Jimmer was more memorable, especially later when he began to make a name for himself on the court.

When Jimmer used to tell kids he met at games what his name was, they would say: "Your name is *WHAT?!*" But by the time they left the court, they all knew Jimmer's name and didn't forget it.

Jimmer's older sister Lindsay initially refused to use it. "I called him James," she recalled. "But the name Jimmer grew on me."

Located 200 miles due north of Manhattan, Glens Falls is a city with less than 15,000 residents. It's the kind of place where neighbors still watch out for one another, front doors go unlocked, people work hard, and close-knit families are the norm. Kay and her husband Al had both grown up in the area and passed those small town values on to their children. A thoroughly modern town, Glens Falls also retains the colonial charm of its past.

Several years ago, *Look Magazine* wrote a series of articles about Glens Falls, calling it Hometown U.S.A. because it represented the heart of America. The accompanying photos depicted parents walking arm in arm, freckle-faced children eating ice cream cones and riding through town on scooters — the kind of place many people, like Jimmer's parents, think ideal to settle in and raise a family.

Al Fredette and Kay Taft grew up 25 miles away from Glens Falls in Whitehall, New York, a former colonial settlement on Lake Champlain known as the birthplace of the United States Navy. Sport has always been a big part of their lives. They met as students at Whitehall High School where Al was a basketball and football star. Kay's fa-

Chip off the Old Block

ther, Clint Taft, was a longtime coach at Whitehall and later served as athletic director at the high school. Kay's brother Jim played basketball at Central Connecticut University and Al played football there, but neither were good enough to pursue a professional career. Instead, he and Kay got married, settled in Glens Falls, and started a family.

Al is a die-hard basketball fan. He played pickup basketball, organized youth leagues and tournaments, and coached in the community. Glens Falls was the place to be if you loved basketball. Its Civic Center became the home of New York's high school basketball state tournament for over 20 years and also hosted USBL pro team games.

For a while Al ran The Fredette Bakery, but the business went under before Jimmer was born, leaving the family in debt and forcing Al to find a new career. He got a job as a financial advisor and Kay worked as a part time teacher, earning enough for a modest lifestyle.

"That wasn't a choice, that was reality," his brother T.J. said, remembering how he and Jimmer slept on side by side mattresses in a small upstairs bedroom. "We didn't have money, that's for sure."

Even so, the Fredette children grew up active and happy, Lindsay recalled, saying their house was "the center of the neighborhood. Everyone was always outside playing sports and games. We were always playing something. My brothers and I always supported each other in what we liked to do, going to games and concerts."

According to the family, from the time Jimmer could walk he was a bundle of competitive energy.

"My mom did not know what to do with his energy," Lindsay said. "So she hooked a chain into the ceiling with a ring on the end, and let Jimmer swing through the living room like a little Tarzan. Jimmer could get it going so he could loop all the way around in a circle through the living room. He even put a hole in the wall once.

"He was always going, and active, getting himself into whatever sport or game was going on around him."

The youngest of three children — Lindsay was born in 1980 and T.J. in 1982. Jimmer was close to both siblings growing up, despite the age differences. He would regularly tag along with T.J. to the basketball court.

"He was the most determined, competitive four-year-old I had ever seen," T.J. said. "He willed himself to find ways to win, even if he was physically outmatched."

Even though he was short and chunky, he was also fearless when taking on the bigger boys. Playing with T.J. and his brother's friends on the Fredette's backyard court, Jimmer developed a long

Chip off the Old Block

range shot and made his first three-pointer when he was five.

Jimmer and T.J. played nearly every day, with Al often acting as referee. Most of the time, T.J. won handily. Being much taller, it was easy for him to block most of Jimmer's shots. So Al instituted a rule where if Jimmer was in the lane, T.J. could block his shot; but if Jimmer stayed on the perimeter, T.J. had to let him shoot. So in the beginning Jimmer stayed on the outside and continued to develop his jump shot.

Al recalled how one evening Jimmer entered the lane and got frustrated when T.J. blocked yet another shot and left the court pouting. After kicking the fence, he came back to play some more. Feeling sorry for his little brother, T.J. backed off defensively. Jimmer stopped dribbling and raised his hand, indicating he wanted his brother to guard him full on.

"Don't go easy on me, is what he meant," T.J. laughed. "For a kid that was five years old to be that competitive, you could see that it was something that would set him apart."

To navigate through T.J.'s defense when driving to the hoop, Jimmer learned the head fakes, scoop shots, and floaters that would one day become his signature moves.

Jimmer's whole family encouraged his passion for basketball. Kay built a small dribbling studio in the basement with mirrors on the wall so he could see his form. Kay's brother Lee, a professional personal trainer, had his nephew running drills when he was just five. Years later Jimmer would note, "I wouldn't be where I am today without him. He's the reason I move as well as I do."

When Jimmer was little, he and a few of his buddies would go to Lee's garage where they'd train for an hour or more. When he was in the sixth and seventh grades, he started to pick it up a little bit, making the workouts more intense.

"He set a goal at a young age and that is rare," Lee said. You get a lot of young people who say they want to play in the NBA, NFL, or Major League Baseball — that is just talk. But Jimmer took action all the time.

Lindsay also spent time with Jimmer, shagging his rebounds for hours at a time. "I kept asking him, *When are you going to be done?* because I was getting dizzy just looking for the ball," she admitted. "I actually enjoyed it because it was a good workout for me. I'd rebound for him and sometimes I would do crazy things like get in his face and yell and scream as a joke. Then I'd say, 'Hey, you've got to be able to handle that.' I liked to help him out and I tease him that it's my rebounding and defensive skills that got him to where he is today, but definitely T.J. was the one who helped him with his actual skills and develop his craft."

Jimmer agreed. "I wanted to be like him at

Chip off the Old Block

such a young age that I think it helped me with my development."

When he was eight years old, Jimmer would play adult pick-up games at a local park with Al and T.J. He also participated in Hoop It Up tournaments, three-on-three contests, and later traveled to New York City for no-foul blacktop games that Al believed "toughened him up" mentally as much as physically because it wasn't just his chubbiness and his smaller stature he had to overcome. Al believes some people may have looked at Jimmer differently, or considered him somehow lacking, because he followed a less conventional religion for the area.

When Al was 18, he followed in his older brother's footsteps and converted to The Church of Jesus Christ of Latter-day Saints. Kay was raised a Catholic, and they agreed to let their children decide what religion they wanted to follow. Jimmer and his siblings all chose to become Latter-day Saints (informally called Mormons), while Kay remains a practicing Catholic. Unlike Utah, where a little over 60 percent of the population is Mormon, there were not many in their community.

Nevertheless, there were a few kids his age in the local congregation, Jimmer said. "We had fun together."

But there was nobody he had as much fun with as T.J., who made practicing something to look forward to. For example, T.J. had Jimmer pretend every free throw attempt was for a big game.

"He'd make so many in a row that I had to make stuff up," T.J. smiled. "*O.K., now you're playing at the Olympics. Now you make this shot, and you feed all the people in the world.* From the time he was 10, I was telling everybody he was going to make the NBA."

T.J. also described Jimmer's competitiveness as being "off the charts. It was just crazy. I thought, *I gotta capitalize on this. He's got something special.*" T.J. promised himself he would do whatever he could to enable his brother to reach his full potential.

Both Lindsay and T.J. were role models for Jimmer. T.J. played point guard for the Glens Falls High School team. Lindsay also participated in sports, was a good student, and played the violin. When she was 18, Lindsay won the Miss New York Teen USA Pageant. She later toured as a member of a premier modern dance group.

In addition to basketball, T.J. pursued music enthusiastically — and fearlessly. When T.J. was a senior in high school, a friend suggested he try his hand at writing some rhymes. Rapping quickly became a passion. He would get gigs at local hardcore rock clubs, rapping to a predominantly heavy metal crowd. He developed a rap style that steered clear of edgy, profane-laced lyrics. Nor was it at all preachy.

Chip off the Old Block

"A lot of it with me isn't really religious," T.J. explained. "My mother ... would not let us swear in the house. I just grew up not really talking that way. I put my experiences in my life into music, into words, and I don't speak that way — I try to make a conscious effort not to do that."

Al made sure of it. "I would hear him and his friends in the basement and they'd be rapping," he said. "They'd come up and say, Mr. Fredette, you should go down and listen to T.J. — he's really good."

Al told him: "As long as you keep the standards that we're not going to have off-color in our house. That was difficult in the beginning, because everything you listened to in the rap world was different than what T.J. was doing."

In 2003, Rap-A-Lot Records requested to hear his demos, and then asked for more. But the hoped-for offer never materialized. Despite the disappointment, T.J. forged ahead, forming a group called the Designated Hittazs, many of whom had grown up in Brooklyn or the Bronx before moving upstate. The group wrote their own music and performed at gigs all across the state. But a record deal eluded them, and after a couple of years, the group decided to disband and pursue solo careers. The split was amicable and they made a pact that whoever made it big first would be there to help the others.

Al believes his children succeeded because they

were raised in an environment that valued a work ethic. "Our neighbors, the community, the area — we had to work and work hard."

Jimmer applied that same mindset to basketball, and for as good as he already was, that persistence was going to make him even better.

Most people have that one special teacher that they feel a special attachment to. For Jimmer, it was his kindergarten teacher, Leslee Bickford at the Sanford Street Elementary School in Glens Falls. Every year from first grade on, he would stop in to visit Ms. Bickford, who has been one of his most staunch supporters over the years.

In June 2011, Jimmer made his last trip to the Sanford Street School, which was being closed by the local school district. He and T.J. spoke to the students in an assembly, reminiscing about their time at Sanford Street. When T.J. was in the first grade, he did an Elvis impersonation at a Sunshine Assembly. Jimmer, who still holds the school record for the triple jump, played on his first basketball team in the third grade. He also treated his audience to a ball handling display, effortlessly dribbling two basketballs up and down the court, through his legs and back.

"This is the exact gym right here that we used to practice in every single day," he told the students. "This is where the journey started, and I've just worked hard ever since."

Jimmer is also quick to credit his family. "My

Chip off the Old Block

dad was my coach up until sixth or seventh grade. He's been a huge influence on my life basketball-wise and as far as being a good kid. My brother would always work with me no matter what. He'd never say, *No, I don't have the time.* And my mother just always told me, *You can reach any dreams you have.*"

T.J. stressed the importance of determination to the awe-struck students. "Anything you guys want — you can achieve your dreams."

All the proof they needed was standing right in front of them.

3 Team Sports

By the time Jimmer joined his first basketball team in third grade, he already played at a higher level than others his age. Eric Medved, who later coached Jimmer in the Amateur Athletic Union (AAU), credits the Fredette family. "The start that he got on his path to success was certainly laid with a strong foundation that was taught by his father Al, and many of his family members along the way. Having coached Jimmer, I can tell you that he has a cerebral way about his handling of the game. He has the uncanny ability of being able to walk onto a court, size-up his competition, and then determine as a game is going on, which of the myriad of ways he is going to beat you."

When T.J. earned a spot on his high school basketball team, Jimmer worked as the team's water boy. During halftime, he would entertain the crowd by going on the court and making shot after shot. His Pillsbury Doughboy stature made his athleticism that much more unexpected.

"Halftime, it was my specialty," Jimmer said. "I was a little chubby back then, so it was probably funny to watch the chubby kid keep making shots."

T.J. had been Glens Falls' star point guard, leading his team to the state semifinals in 1999 and the Section II semifinals in 2000. After graduating, he enrolled at Adirondack Community College in nearby Queensbury and led its basketball team in scoring during the 2001-02 season. He was also a great playmaker — averaging near 5 assists per game.

The two years he played at ACC would be the end of T.J.'s academic sports career. While he still played in night leagues, he channeled his basketball dreams into Jimmer, taking on role of personal trainer, coach, cheerleader, and mentor.

T.J. was constantly thinking up new drills. When Jimmer was 10, T.J. had him wear heavy work gloves while practicing his dribble on the small cement patio in their backyard and with T.J. trying to push him off the patio and onto the grass.

"My dad actually yelled at me for that," T.J. recalled, "because he came home one day and we were doing it when it was really hot. He said, *You gotta stop. You're going to kill him.*"

"It had to be 95 degrees out," Al said, "and I was worried. But T.J. just said, 'He'll be fine.' I said, 'OK, just make sure you give him some water.'" But Al also knows that T.J.'s pushing Jimmer's limits were important. "That's where he learned to be confident. He learned from his older brother and still does. They're responsible for each other and I think we're only seeing the early stages of this."

T.J. called another one of his drills *The Gauntlet*. T.J. would take Jimmer to the Latter-day Saints church in nearby Queensbury, which had a long, dark hallway. Jimmer had to dribble mostly by feel and not rely on looking at the ball. When he mastered that, T.J. invited some of his friends along, who would randomly jump out of doorways, forcing Jimmer to use crossover dribbles and spin moves to avoid them. If Jimmer lost the ball, he'd have to start over.

A drawback of extramural school sports is that they have clearly defined seasons. But since basketball was a year-round passion for Jimmer, he needed to find other outlets. So from the time he started playing on the Sanford Street team, Jimmer also played on off-season teams in the AAU, including the Wilton Hornets, Northeast Sharks, and the Albany City Rocks. In seventh grade, his Hornets team finished their season 24-0 and then played in the national tournament.

While still in eighth grade, Jimmer and his best friend Denny Wilhelm were promoted to the Glens Falls High School varsity team during sectionals. "It was just great to work against them in practice," Jimmer said. Their coach, Tony Hammel, said he wanted them to "get a taste of what it's like to get to that level" since he was hoping they'd do the same thing the next year.

Coach Hammel knew Jimmer was a special player at that time because of his scoring ability and his work ethic.

The team won their section, went to regionals, and then made it to the state tournament finals — finishing the season 27-1.

"Seeing the Civic Center so packed with that team was amazing." Jimmer said. "If we work hard enough, we can contend for a state title, too."

Through the AAU league, Jimmer met others who were just as focused on basketball as he was. He got to know future Penn State University star Talor Battle when he hit the winning shot in overtime the day eighth-grade Jimmer scored 51 points in the Northeast Stars' loss to the Albany City Rocks. They developed a close friendship and rivalry that would last through high school and college.

Albany coach Jim Hart, who later convinced Jimmer to play for the City Rocks, remembered: "He looked like a little fat kid, and he was absolutely destroying an inner-city team."

4 "He's a Freshman!"

In his first game on the varsity team as a freshman, Jimmer had two three-pointers and scored 13 points coming off the bench. He scored 10 in his second game. He later had games of 25, 27 and 22 points and finished the regular season with 27 three-pointers — emerging as a proven scoring threat.

Jimmer said the upperclassmen on the team welcomed the freshmen but stressed the importance of putting the team first and individual statistics second. "They'd congratulate us as much as they'd tell us to work harder," which was never an issue with Jimmer.

Although freshmen traditionally did not start (nor even play) on the Glens Falls Indians' varsity basketball team, Coach Hammel made Jimmer a starter during the season after having to bench one of the older players for disciplinary reasons.

In his first sectional tournament game, he had four assists, six three-pointers and set his new career-high with 32 points. He drove the baseline and hit a layup to give them a one point win. They lost in the Class A sectional quarterfinals and the Indians finished their season 16-6. Jimmer was the team's second-leading scorer and was selected for the Foothills Council All Stars First Team.

Perhaps the most important outcome was that Jimmer became more confident in his game and in his team's collective ability, which carried over to the next season when he told a local reporter that he believed the Indians were good enough to win the state championship — even though the team had four sophomore starters. He also had his sights set on becoming the team's all-time leading scorer.

"There's a lot I want to do here," he told the reporter. "We have the guys to do it and we also have the time. Not a single day goes by that I don't think about it."

"He puts a lot of time into making himself better," Coach Hammel said. "He sets goals for himself, which not too many kids do anymore. He realizes what his weaknesses are. One of his big weaknesses early on was speed, and he worked on that with [his uncle] Lee Taft's program."

Lee calls his nephew "extremely powerful. And he has an ability when he's in the air, when he takes contact or is spinning, to know exactly where his body is spatially. He knows where the ground is. He almost has catlike instincts. It might look like he's off balance, but he's really not."

Although Jimmer started to grow and lose his baby fat in high school, it was clear he would never be overly tall or burly — he was clearly a guard and would never be a power forward. Precisely because of that, T.J. knew it was important that Jimmer knew how to take a body check.

"T.J. would say, *you have to get used to contact. You are a sturdy kid, but you have to be able to go strong to the hoop and score,*" Jimmer said. "So I would drive into the lane and he would hit me or foul me hard. I would have to make five straight shots while being hit, or he would make me do it over again."

Those who lived in and around Glens Falls had long believed Jimmer was something special on the basketball court but beginning in 2004, he began to make a name for himself beyond the confines of his hometown. Playing for the Northeast Sharks, he was voted onto the All-GymRat Challenge Team. This tournament held every Memorial Day weekend in the Albany, New York area featured teams from across North America. Evaluators rated him "the top outside-shooter in the 15-and-under tournament with endless range, a lightning quick release and the ability to hit shots with defenders in his face." It was noted that he could play point guard or shooting guard, he rebounded well, and that he didn't "shy away from a defensive challenge."

Two months after those props, Jimmer was the leading scorer and made the All Tournament Team at the Reebok Big Time Tournament in Las Vegas, America's largest summer basketball tournament. His scoring average of 29.3 points is one of their top all-time single tournament scoring records (and only a tenth of a point from the legendary Kobe Bryant's average).

5 Motivation

While he may have spent more time playing basketball than any other activity, Jimmer was not a one sport athlete. At 12, he could hit home runs of 350 feet and he was also a talented wide receiver in football. Wearing jersey number 32, Jimmer wasn't the fastest or tallest but he always seemed to be the craftiest receiver on the field, knowing how to use his body to ward off defenders and catch the ball.

Jimmer grew up playing football and it was more of a social activity than basketball. "We always played football in his backyard, and it was a small backyard — that's where he picked up his little moves," his friend Denny recalled. "We'd play two-hand touch and he'd run back a kick, and no one would get two hands on him."

A natural athlete, Jimmer made the junior varsity football team as a sophomore, playing wide receiver as well as outside linebacker. Five football games into the season, he was brought up to the Indians varsity team to replace an injured player. Within a few games, he became a key player and finished the season as one of the division's top running backs — earning Second Team All-Star honors.

When the school basketball season began, Jimmer backed up his lofty goals on the court. In the opening game of his sophomore season, he had 32 points, including four three-pointers, leading Glens Falls to victory. The team featured several sophomores including four starters. "We're really stepping it up and playing as a team because we always play a lot together in AAU and everything," Jimmer said.

The Indians opened the season with ten straight wins, with Jimmer averaging 28.6 points per game.

Coach Hammel admitted, "I'm a little surprised about the start we had, but these kids take it in stride. You really don't have to worry about these kids. They're smart. As far as Jimmer goes, as a sophomore, he's ahead of almost everyone we've had here recently when they were his age. And when you think about the players we've had, that's saying a lot."

The team continued to overachieve into the playoffs. In the Section II Class A quarterfinal, Jimmer scored 16 points in the fourth quarter and made three steals to lead Glens Falls to a thrilling 59-57 victory. He was also perfect from the free throw line in the final eight minutes of the game. He tied the game on a foul shot with 25 seconds remaining and gave the Indians their first lead since

Motivation

early in the first quarter with just 13.3 seconds left.

After the game Jimmer acknowledged: "This was the biggest game I've been in so far. I've played a lot of AAU ball where I've had to do something like that, but there were not quite as many fans, and it's not as big a stage as this is right here."

There would be no fairytale ending to the Indians' season, though. A week later, Jimmer had a chance to tie the score on free throws with 1.9 seconds left. He made the first basket to bring the team within one point. But the second free throw hit the heel of the rim and bounced out into an opponent's waiting hands, giving Burnt Hills the Section II championship.

"That's a lot of pressure to put on anyone, in this game, in this building," Coach Hammel said. "Jimmer's the type of kid that wants that shot and he'll take it over and over again. Unfortunately, this one didn't fall."

Hammel was right — rather than get down on himself and go into a funk, Jimmer used that miss to motivate himself to do better.

"We wanted to get to the Civic Center," he said, reflecting on the loss. "We're young and we'll be in this spot again. You use something like this for drive so when you come back next year, you're head and shoulders above the rest. And we believe that."

Jimmer had averaged 27 points per game and was recognized as All-Foothills Council First Team and Class A All-State Fifth Team.

Jimmer gained more attention at the 2005 Gym-Rat Challenge when he was named the Most Valuable Player on the AAU circuit.

In a write up on Jimmer's performance, a sportswriter noted: "Unique name, superior game. This performer truly personifies the phrase, *looks can be deceiving*. If Fredette walked up to any open run, he almost always would be one of the last players picked. This sharp-shooting whiz kid makes anyone who takes him lightly [on defense] pay a heavy price. ... but Fredette is much more than merely a perimeter assassin. Not only does Fredette elevate the level of the players around him, he also comes through in the clutch when his team needs him the most."

Jimmer scored 22 points in the semifinals and 25 points in the championship game. He finished the tournament with 15 three-pointers and led his team with a 17 point per game average.

John Kmack, the director of the GymRat Challenge, later recalled, "I remember Jimmer telling me this one time during the tournament [that] every time he stepped on the floor, he believed he was the best player there. That year, there was an unbelievable amount of talent there — Kemba Walker [who later won a NCAA championship with the University of Connecticut and

Motivation

plays for the Charlotte Bobcats] and Cole Aldrich [who later played at the University of Kansas and the Oklahoma City Thunder] were there and Jimmer is the one that captured the attention. You can't help but be a believer."

Kmack also admitted that watching Jimmer mature as a player from elementary to high school had been this side of amazing. "He looked like Joey-bag-of-donuts with feet that were too big. ... There are very few players that have maximized their abilities like Jimmer. He is just fun to watch."

While Jimmer was in Houston for an AAU tournament, Al approached a Brigham Young University coach who was watching the game in the stands. He introduced himself as a Mormon and let the coach know that his son planned to attend the BYU camp that summer.

Besides being a LDS school, it was also Lindsay's alma mater. She had graduated from BYU with a degree in modern dance. She still lived in Utah with her husband and worked as a school teacher so going to camp was a chance to spend time near his big sister.

At camp, it didn't take long for the Brigham Young coaches to have Jimmer scrimmaging with BYU players, who worked as camp counselors. It was from that camp that Jimmer's name made its way onto the university's recruitment wish list. But as he entered his junior year of high school,

Beyond the Arc

Jimmer's attention was focused on getting his team to the state final.

6 Working Out

A solid football player as a sophomore, he had a breakout year in his junior year, including an 87-yard touchdown return of the opening kickoff against eventual state champion Amsterdam. In that game, which Glens Falls won 33-27, Jimmer accounted for 300 all-purpose yards and three touchdowns. For the season, he caught a Section II-best 43 passes for 910 yards and scored 15 total touchdowns in nearly every way possible: catching passes, returning kickoffs and punts, and recovering fumbles on defense.

Jimmer's friend Denny was the football team's quarterback. "I think the more we're together, the more we'll be good together in any sport," Jimmer said. "I know what he's thinking, and he knows what I'm thinking. So I think our being together in basketball definitely helps out here [on the football field]."

Denny believed Jimmer would have been just as good regardless of who was quarterback. "I remember him being just a straight-out athlete. I could put the ball anywhere and he'd catch it. He's one of the most gifted athletes I've ever known. He still is a lot quicker and faster than people give him credit for. He's also the most focused kid you'll ever meet. I'm blessed to know him as my best friend. He's the same kid he was in kindergarten — he hasn't changed, and that's a good thing."

Glens Falls football coach, Pat Lilac, calls Jimmer explosive. "I don't know how many five yard hitch routes he turned into 70-yard touchdowns. He doesn't look like he's running that fast, but he moves with such body control and smoothness it's deceptive. The most important thing was his competitiveness and his will to win. He always had a knack for making big plays."

Jimmer earned Player of the Year honors in football for the *The Post-Star* All-Star team. He was also named an all-state receiver and outside linebacker, which sparked interest in him from Penn State and other college football programs. Every Ivy League school sent a letter asking to sit down with him. Jimmer was flattered but politely declined because while he enjoyed football, basketball remained his primary focus — and joy.

The Indians basketball team started their season strong with 16 wins. Jimmer averaged 30 points per game, but was also getting lots of assists. "If you hit the open guys, things will open up for you too" was Jimmer's philosophy about passing.

One of the things that made Jimmer fun to

Working Out

watch was the obvious pleasure he took in playing, whether in front of a raucous home team or partisan away crowd, in a high school game or AAU competition.

Kevin Kucel, who was Jimmer's teammate in the under-12 AAU division and played against him in high school, remembers how much Jimmer enjoyed playing in his old Gloversville High School gym. "He loved coming here and playing in the smaller gym with the fans right on top of you. He knew coming here our fans were going to be all over him. He kind of liked that and fed off it. They used to get after him but they also had a respect for him as well."

"Honestly, I feel more comfortable on the road," Jimmer said. "I take the heckling as a compliment." He said the hush that falls over an opponent's home crowd when he hits a three is his "favorite sound."

But, Kucel stressed: "He was always respectful and I think everyone respected him for that. When some kids get that good they get to be more arrogant, but that is not him on or off the court."

Gloversville coach Don Landrio observed: "Certainly, he had a lot of skills and he handled the ball well. He made the players around him much better and his shooting ability was outstanding." But most of all, Landrio said, was that Jimmer had "a great attitude. He was a good winner and when he lost he was a good loser."

Jimmer also encouraged constructive criticism. "I'm always trying to get people to critique my game. If I really want to be a great player, I'm not going to go out and shoot 100 layups that I know I'm going to make. I'm going to work on parts of the game I really need to improve."

Despite his ability to almost score at will, Jimmer made a conscious effort not to ball hog and to keep his teammates involved. "If I have an open shot, I'm going to take it, but if I don't, I'm going to run the offense and work for something better. They say the great players try to make their teammates better, like Bird and Magic."

Another coach, Scott Hale of Johnstown High School, observed that Jimmer's looks could be deceiving. "When he walked into the gym you wouldn't think he was a very good basketball player, but when he stepped between the lines he was unbelievable but also a very respectful kid. He was very modest."

Hale recalled the first time he experienced *Jimmer Time*, during Jimmer's junior year. "It was a close game going into the fourth quarter and we were ahead. He just took over in the fourth quarter, and they went on to win. I heard all these sports commentators questioning his game, his athleticism, and his lack of ability to play defense... they are wrong. He is very athletic, used his body very well, and when he needed to dig in and play defense, he certainly did."

Working Out

Jimmer continued to work out. His Uncle Lee introduced olympic lifting and a little more explosive weightlifting. Jimmer's jumping ability started to come and he got stronger and more physical. "As his body got more ready," Lee said, "I upped the ante a little bit and made him train harder."

As he grew taller and leaner, Jimmer's ball mastery also steadily improved. His elevated skills did not go unnoticed. As one local sports writer observed:

"Fredette is making those same shots while being double-teamed, passing with pinpoint accuracy and making steals on unsuspecting guards. The now 6-foot-1 guard even dunked on a breakaway recently."

The Indians finished their regular season with a 19-1 record. In the first game in the Section II playoffs, they were matched up with Burnt Hills who ended their season the previous year. Jimmer had six assists as the Indians cruised to victory. In the semifinal, played at the Civic Center, he scored their first 14 points and outscored the competition 10-0 leading to another huge win.

Their high octane offense was averaging 70.6 points per game, but in the Class A final against Averill Park they scored a season-low of 51 points. After scoring 33 points and hitting five threes, it came down to Jimmer's last shot. "They set up the inbounds play for me and I was able to get the shot off," he said. "I just missed it."

For the season, he had scored over 30 points thirteen times and was named the MVP of the Foothills Council and to the New York All-State Class A Boys Basketball Team.

In the off-season, the Indians played in the Catch A Rising Star showcase in Pennsylvania, highlighting many of the Northeast's top teams. Jimmer was named the most valuable player after averaging 30 points per game — and his team won the 64-team tournament. Coach Hammel knew then that his team would be special the upcoming year.

That summer, Jimmer and Denny also continued to play AAU ball with the Albany City Rocks in national-caliber tournaments throughout the United States. Their team finished third in the 17-and-under National Tournament against teams filled with the top ranked incoming seniors in the country. They were the first team representing New York to ever advance that far in the tourney. In one game, their team was down by 15 with six minutes left — from that point on Jimmer didn't miss a shot and helped orchestrate a huge comeback.

"We're playing teams full of elite Division I players, and we had a shot at the title," commented City Rocks head coach Tim Moseman after the event ended. "Playing in front of two or three

Working Out

thousand people and all these D1 coaches — it was an amazing atmosphere."

He called Jimmer's performance unbelievable. "His shooting ability is incredible. He can shoot it from almost half-court, and if you come out on him, he'll go by you or make a pass. He scores quiet points, too — he'll score 30, 34 points and you wonder how he did it. It's amazing how he takes the game over in the fourth quarter. He steps up his game to another level."

7 Recruitment

It is not unusual for colleges to start recruiting highly ranked high school athletes in their junior year, hoping to get commitment as early as possible. Jimmer started receiving around four letters per day and heard from Syracuse, Massachusetts, Virginia Tech, West Virginia, Lehigh, Utah, Marshall, Virginia, Siena, American, Notre Dame, Georgetown, Utah State, Georgia Tech, Fairfield, and other schools.

Jimmer was hoping to get a scholarship offer from an elite program, such as Syracuse University, which was just a two hour drive from Glens Falls. Surprisingly, though, only a relative handful of major programs offered Jimmer a scholarship, despite him averaging over 29 points a game is junior year.

Syracuse assistant coach Mike Hopkins said it wasn't a case of not wanting him for their basketball program; it was that they were already shooting guard heavy.

"It was one of those things where we didn't want to take too many," he explained. "Jimmer's one of those guys who you look back ... and well, we all make mistakes. But us not signing him wasn't by any stretch because he couldn't play."

Syracuse's decision not to offer Jimmer a scholarship prompted Hopkins' friend Dave Rose, who is BYU's head basketball coach, to ask if it was because he hadn't heard of Jimmer. Hopkins laughed.

"I told Dave, *the kid's a joke* — and I mean that in a good way. Jimmer knew where everybody was on the floor. He had intelligence, savvy, obviously could shoot it. He could put on a show. People knew him, and knew he was interested in BYU."

Kurt Kanaskie, Penn State University assistant basketball coach, agreed that Jimmer was considered a high-level recruit although he noted: "The knock on him was always that he may not be quick or strong enough."

But the main reason for the apparent lack of interest, said Kanaskie, was that it was assumed it was pretty much a given that Jimmer was heading west.

Jimmer's AAU teammate, Talor Battle, who became a star at PSU (and later played professionally in Europe) said: "Everyone was pretty sure he was going to either BYU or Utah, being Mormon. He's really into his religion."

While his faith is important, so is his family and the decision to move 2000 miles away was not made lightly. Had it not been for Lindsay living in

Recruitment

Utah, Jimmer might have chosen a school closer to home, such as Siena or Massachusetts.

"Knowing there was family out here to support him allowed him to make that decision," Lindsay said.

She told her brother about her experiences with classes, roommates, the fun things to do on campus, and unique things that are part of the BYU environment. "It ties in with our faith," she said. "But I never told him go to BYU. I didn't try to sway him. He's a really good decision-maker. He listens to people but he doesn't let it sway his core beliefs. He makes really good decisions, then sticks to it."

The BYU recruiters did everything in their power to convince Jimmer to decide in their favor, frequently traveling back east to scout him. Al called the school's commitment to Jimmer "amazing," recalling how Coach Rose once showed up for one of Jimmer's football games. To get to Glens Falls from Provo, Rose had to catch a flight into Cincinnati, connect to an Albany flight, and then drive an hour.

Rose said he was hoping "that when it came down to the end of that process, because there were many, many big-time schools and coaches who came through the gyms and watched those games, that we'd still be around."

Al said Rose's doggedness definitely impressed his son and when it came time to visit prospective schools, BYU was first on Jimmer's list. He toured the campus in early September 2006 and was impressed with the school as well as the coaches and players he met. He also visited Siena but opted against touring Marshall.

After Jimmer's visit to Provo, Rose and first assistant coach John Wardenburg visited the Fredettes in Glens Falls. "We went out to dinner, went back home and talked, and the coaches showed us videos of the school and the team," Jimmer recalled.

In the end, it was a family decision, based on what school would be the best fit academically. "It was a chance to play basketball at a high level and maybe to contribute right away," Jimmer said. "It was a chance to go where people believe in the same things that I do."

So within a week of visiting Provo, Jimmer made a verbal commitment to attend BYU, then signed his letter of intent in early November, receiving a full scholarship and the possibility of starting sometime his freshman year.

"That's one of the main reasons I'm going to the school," Jimmer said. "They know I can shoot and they want me to shoot, so they can move me out to the two in situations, but I think it will be more running the point."

Coach Hammel believes Jimmer made the right decision, in part because of the academics. "It's a school that fits the young man and his character.

Recruitment

It's a big decision for him and I'm sure it's a big relief for him and his family."

If there was any trepidation on Jimmer's part, it was the idea of being so far away from Glens Falls. "Being away from my family, having them so far away. I've always been around here. But I'll be playing basketball, so I'm sure I'll meet people easier and that'll help."

Now that the distraction of recruitment was over, Jimmer looked forward to his senior season and getting one last chance to lead Glens Falls to a state championship.

8 Senior Season!

Once his college choice was made, Jimmer felt a responsibility to the BYU program and informed his football coach he was opting out of his senior year. "Some people in town were upset I didn't play," he acknowledged. "But I felt like I owed it to BYU not to get hurt."

Jimmer hit five three-pointers and scored 32 points to win in the first game of his 2006-07 senior season and in his second game he had 44 points with 11 free throws in the fourth quarter. The Indians also started strong.

In December 2006, during the Coaches vs. Cancer Shootout benefit, Glens Falls High School honored Jimmer for becoming the school's all time leading scorer. As a junior, he had averaged 29.4 points per game and eclipsed Jim Town's record of 1,599 points, which had stood for more than 30 years. During the ceremony, Town presented Jimmer with a commemorative basketball as the pair received a rousing standing ovation. Later, Jimmer expressed admiration for Town's humility.

"Someone would say something about how good he was and he'd laugh and say *I'm not as good as that*. He was just a very level-headed, humble, and down-to-earth guy, and when I get to his age, I'd like to be like that." As far as surpassing Town, Jimmer was philosophical. "That record will be there, but enjoying the game is what keeps you going."

Coach Hammel said Jimmer showed flashes of brilliance many times, but one game that particularly stuck out was against Scotia. His 11 fourth-quarter points came at just the right time. They trailed most of the game and were down ten points when he took over. He tied the game with a great one-on-one move and a jaw-dropping underhand scoop shot with 1.4 seconds left. In the final minute of overtime, he had another scoop shot and finished the win with 32 points and seven assists.

"What can you say? We don't draw up those plays at the end of the game that forced overtime," Coach Hammel said. "He does that by himself."

A week later, Jimmer reached 2,000 points. The officials temporarily stopped the game as the crowd cheered.

Despite the praise and attention, Jimmer would soon realize that being a big fish in a little sports pond didn't guarantee success on the national stage. If he wanted to extend his playing career into college success and beyond, he'd have to keep proving himself.

To that end, T.J. asked Jimmer "is your goal

still to play in the NBA?" and had Jimmer sign a contract that stated:

I, James T Fredette, agree on this day Jan 27, 2007 to do the work and make the necessary sacrifices to be able to reach my ultimate goal of playing in the NBA.

T.J. also signed it as the witness.

"The first thing you have to do when you have a goal is write it down," Jimmer said. "And that's what we did. I put it right above my bed, and I looked at it every day when I woke up. And it just reminded me that that is what I wanted to do. I loved it, and it kept me motivated to reach that goal."

Soon the Indians clinched the Foothills Council title. In one game, Jimmer had six steals and a breakaway dunk. In another game, he hit five three-pointers and singlehandedly outscored the competition 37 to 35.

A few days later, he set his new career-high with 46 points from 18-for-21 shooting despite leaving the game early in a blowout win. "He was on," Coach Hammel said about his nine three-pointers. "And they weren't short shots, either."

"We knew if we kept going with it and kept working at it, we could win a state title," Jimmer explained on the eve of their semifinal game. "This has been our goal since then."

The game was a thriller, with Glens Falls coming from behind to beat McKinley of Buffalo in the Class A semifinals. Trailing with 46 seconds left in the third quarter, Jimmer hit a three-pointer which pulled his team within one point. With that basket, Jimmer also broke the Section II career scoring record. His heroics seemed to give Glens Falls an adrenaline boost and they outscored McKinley 28-8 in the fourth quarter and won the game 72-54.

"This is probably the best feeling I've ever had in my life," Jimmer said after the game. "We'll just try to do the same thing [in the final]."

This was something he had dreamt about since he was in third grade, when the core group of the current team first played together.

But their season came up short. It started well against defending champion Peekskill, with the Indians jumping out to a 19-14 lead after one quarter. But the Red Devils tightened up their defense, pressuring Glens Falls from the moment they put the ball in play and blocking 10 shots. Jimmer was particularly below his standards, going 3-for-24, including just 2-for-16 from three-point range, as the Red Devils won 58-48 for their third consecutive title.

"We played real well in the first quarter, and we hit a wall in the second quarter," Jimmer said. "I didn't have the greatest shooting night. The shots just didn't fall. But that will happen." Jim-

Senior Season!

mer finished with 19 points, four steals, and seven rebounds.

Although disappointed, Jimmer tried to put the loss in perspective. "It's a little sad because it's the last time you're going to play with your teammates, but I don't mind being second in the state. Many teams would love to be here. This run was just awesome. I wouldn't want to do it with anyone else. The worst part is it being over and not getting to play organized basketball with these guys anymore."

Jimmer finished his high school career with 2,404 points, which placed him sixth on New York's all-time scoring list. He was also named First Team All State by the New York State Sportswriters Association. In his senior year he averaged 29 points a game, scored 30 or more in 12 games, made 81 three-pointers, and shot 92 percent from the free throw line.

To help his brother become even better, T.J. found new challenges and opponents for Jimmer. After Jimmer turned 18, T.J. asked Jimmer if he'd like to go play a game against some prisoners.

For a few years, T.J. and a team of former Glens Falls players played against inmates at nearby correctional facilities. Never one to pass up a new basketball experience, Jimmer agreed and joined

T.J., his father, his uncle, and some friends for a series of pick-up games.

"All the inmates would come in and watch," Jimmer said. "And the guards would be on the sidelines with their guns and everything just so nothing got out of hand."

"The first time I took him there, he scored 40 and when he pulled his first crossover they all went nuts," T.J. recalled. "One of the refs was an inmate. The other was a guard and the prisoners were all circled around the court going crazy."

Jimmer acknowledges there was a "fear factor but it made us more mentally tough just playing in front of inmates like that and the things they would say to you. ... they were just kind of heckling and most of the time they didn't like you at first, but they would start to like us because we played hard, but clean. And you would always have a few guys in there that would be rooting for you or betting that [we] would win so they would be cheering real hard."

In all, Jimmer played five weekends, with his team winning all their games. "It was a great experience."

Jimmer graduated from high school in June and was awarded the U.S. Army Reserve National Scholar-Athlete Award and the Donna Driscoll Memorial Scholarship.

9 Transition

While Jimmer's abilities had earned him a scholarship to college, all the recognitions and achievements in high school and AAU play meant little once he arrived in Provo. They did not guarantee him a starting spot on the team or strike fear in the hearts of his opponents. In many ways he was starting from scratch, having to prove himself all over again. Just how far he had to go was driven home the first day of conditioning training.

Jimmer arrived at BYU carrying 210 pounds on his 6'2" frame. While he may have had quick reflexes on the court, on a running track he was plodding, unable to run a six minute mile and admitted he felt like he was dying by the end of the training session. It was the beginning of a challenging, and sometimes frustrating, learning curve.

On top of that, there was the adjustment of being so far away from his family.

"He was homesick for the first little while," his sister Lindsay recalled. "But he could call me and I could visit him and we could get together. I think it made the transition smoother. He felt like he wasn't alone. That was important as he was trying to be part of a team and transition from high school to college basketball. It was important for him to have that extra support."

By the time the season started, Jimmer had settled into campus life and was working hard to find his place in BYU's basketball system.

Before playing any games, a pre-season conference poll named him as the top freshman. In the Cougars first three games, Jimmer played around 21 minutes per game averaging 8.7 points, 2.7 assists and 2 steals.

"I'm playing in front of a bigger crowd every home game than I ever did in high school," Jimmer said. "The fans get really into it. They love their basketball at BYU."

Nevertheless, the students live a different culture than other schools' rowdy sports fans. BYU's honor code requires them to use clean language, be well groomed, 'live a chaste and virtuous life,' and abstain from alcohol, tobacco, tea and coffee.

The Cougars had a successful 2007-08 season, leading the Mountain Conference with a 14-2 record and going 27-8 overall, ranking 24th in the nation. In Jimmer's first post-season game, in the Mountain West Conference tournament, he had nine points including two for four from the beyond the arc.

But two days later, they lost to UNLV for the conference title. Coming off the bench he played his most minutes up to that date — 27 minutes — and led BYU with 17 points.

They also lost in the first round of the NCAA Tournament to Texas A&M. Due to another guard's injury, Jimmer played the game's last 34 minutes and had three assists, five rebounds, and ten points.

Typically, young male Mormons leave to be missionaries after turning 19 years old, or at the end of their freshman year. Females, if they choose, can go when they are 21. The mission for males lasts two years; for females it's a year and a half. Although missionary work is strongly encouraged, it is not a requirement. (Former NBA players Shawn Bradley and Mark Madsen both went on missions.) For Jimmer, it was a significant moral dilemma and one he said he prayed extensively about before decided not to do a mission.

He had turned 19 in February 2008. He played well his last game of the season, raising expectations for the following season — unless he chose to leave for his two-year mission.

Jimmer said his faith is "more important to me than being a good basketball player. I love our church. I was thinking about a mission. It is something I talked to my family about a lot." But in the end, he said, "I just felt like I should be here, playing basketball, and obviously it has been a big dream of mine to play professional basketball. So I decided to not go on one, and continue to play basketball. It is not like I try not to spread the word as much as I can through all my successes and everything, though, and people have been really supportive." Also, Jimmer believes he could best represent his Church through basketball. "I've had numerous situations where people have told me they've checked out the religion because they knew who I was and they heard about my religion," he explained.

The season had ended the way it started, with Jimmer a reserve, warming the bench more than he played. He did not start any games, averaging just 18 minutes and seven points per game. It was an important reality check. Jimmer now knew he needed to significantly improve his strength and his conditioning and hone his ball-handling skills even more if he was going to earn a starting spot and keep his NBA dreams on track.

10 Stepping Up

While his seven points a game were respectable, Jimmer knew he had to improve and be ready to carry a greater load in his sophomore year. He worked hard over the summer and returned to BYU in the best shape of his life. The last vestiges of baby fat were gone and Jimmer was now 195 pounds of cut muscle. He ran a 5:36 mile and had a three foot vertical leap.

He started the season strong. Early on he was recognized — for the first time in his college career — as the Mountain West Conference Player of the Week for averaging 20 points per game and shooting over 72 percent from the field and over 87 percent from the free throw line (for the week).

BYU was also playing great and built the nation's longest home-court winning streak to 53 games (over multiple seasons). But in the second largest crowd in Marriott Center history, they lost to the No. 6 ranked Wake Forest.

Now a starter, Jimmer continued to play great with a 21 point, 10 assist double-double at Utah and a new career high of 28 points against

Wyoming — which included eight consecutive points capped off with a dunk.

In his second player of the week honor, he averaged 26.5 points, 3.5 steals, 3.5 assists, and 2.5 rebounds per game — and 14 for 15 from the free throw line.

The Cougars went 25-7 and won the Mountain West Conference regular season title. Jimmer played in every game, starting all but one. He was second on the team in scoring, averaging more than 16 points per game, shooting 39 percent of his three-pointers while adding four rebounds and four assists per game. Beyond his offensive contribution, Jimmer's leadership and confidence were also more evident. He was named First Team All Mountain West, becoming the first Cougar point guard to be so honored in 18 years.

The Cougars were scheduled to play Texas A&M once again in the first round of the West Regional for the NCAA tournament. The games were being played in Philadelphia, close enough to Glens Falls that 40 friends and family had tickets for the game. BYU had not won a NCAA tournament game since 1993 and so the Cougar faithful were hopeful Jimmer could help break that six-game losing streak. But despite leading the team with 18 points, BYU lost the game 79-66.

While the season may have ended, Jimmer's reputation was just heating up.

11 Legend in the Making

The University of Arizona's McKale Center crowd of over 13 thousand was stunned as the BYU squad crushed their team with their worst home loss in 37 years. Jimmer had just hit his ninth three-pointer when his coach pulled him out for the rest of the game. He hugged him and many fans gave him a standing ovation. They had just witnessed a night to remember.

"I was looking at the basket, and it was looking pretty big, and I had a good stroke tonight," Jimmer said after breaking the McKale Center and BYU scoring records. He shot 16-for-23 from the field and finished with 49 points.

His impressive nine assists and seven rebounds that night would be forgotten, but he catapulted into a household name as his performance was highlighted on ESPN's Sports Center.

Sports writers were referring to Jimmer, now a junior in college, as BYU's star point guard and he was considered a top candidate for the Mountain West Conference's Player of the Year — and even as a candidate as a First Team All-America player. Many fans considered him the best player since NBA star Danny Ainge wore a Cougar uniform. BYU's Coach Rose understood the comparison. "Danny had a great BYU career, but what he did after BYU was something pretty special, too. I think that Jimmer is on that path."

However, the season wasn't without frustration. Jimmer was forced to miss games after he contracted mononucleosis in January 2010 then later suffered from a stomach ailment. The affects of his health issues could be seen in the box scores of a couple games when he scored in single digits. But Jimmer quickly bounced back, finishing with a 22.1 points, 4.7 assists per game average, helping push the 14th ranked Cougars to a 30-6 record, the best regular-season in BYU history.

In March 2010, as Jimmer prepared to lead his team into the NCAA tournament, T.J. released a music video he created called "Amazing," which tells the story of the two brothers challenging each other to greatness.

"It was an easy song for me to write because I just had to go back and think of everything," T.J. said. "I could have written 10 songs about it, but I just took the things that were most crucial to the song and put the words to the beat."

T.J.'s message to his little brother was the same as it always had been: "Stay focused. Don't worry about what people are telling you from the out-

Legend in the Making

side. You know what you need to do. Work hard. Work as hard as you possibly can."

Nobody was prouder than T.J. "I can't even put it into words. It's unbelievable," he told a reporter. "I see him play, and it gives me chills sometimes when he hits some of those big shots and the crowd is going crazy."

The cheers were loudest when Jimmer led the Cougars to their first NCAA Tournament win in seventeen years, beating Florida in a double overtime thriller, 99-92. Jimmer led the Cougars with 37 points. But two nights later 7th ranked Kansas State ended the BYU season with an 84-72 win.

Although disappointed, Jimmer didn't have much time to dwell on what might have been. He had a decision to make — whether to stay at BYU for his senior year or make the jump to the NBA. In the spring, he worked out with the Oklahoma City Thunder, New Jersey Nets, New York Knicks, and Boston Celtics. The workouts included individual drills and one-on-one full court games against other hopefuls. (Jimmer had a brief scare during his workout with the Knicks when he strained a quad muscle but it was later deemed a minor injury.) With his NBA dream so close, most assumed he would enter the draft. But once again, Jimmer defied expectations.

In his junior year, Jimmer took more than a third of all the Cougars' shots. But while most fans focused on his scoring, there was more to

Jimmer's game than hitting threes. As teammate Charles Abouo observed: "When it's time to get that win, he makes all kinds of plays besides putting the ball in the basket."

Even so, some NBA team scouts questioned whether Jimmer's overall game was suitable for the pros, an opinion that Jimmer shrugged off. "I've never worried when people have said, *'You can't do it,'* but it does fuel me."

Jimmer's Coach Rose also dismissed the doubters, telling *Sports Illustrated*: "From what I hear, there is a group of teams that really believe in Jimmer. One of those teams is going to pick him. Then a lot of people will see what he's really capable of doing."

According to his dad Al, even though there was a lot of interest in Jimmer: "No one would guarantee a first round pick, but they're not guaranteeing them for anyone. All four teams were surprised in his athleticism."

According to NBA sources, Jimmer's strengths included his shooting ability plus mental and physical toughness. However, there was also a question about whether he had enough athleticism to go strong to the rim in the pros or to maintain his shooting prowess against NBA teams.

Experts projected Jimmer to be a late first round or early second round pick so it wasn't a question of whether or not he would be drafted; the bigger issue was whether leaving school early

Legend in the Making

would be the best move for him personally and professionally. Ultimately, Jimmer decided to return to BYU for his senior year and use another college season to improve his game even more and increase his draft appeal.

Later in the summer, he had the opportunity to play with NBA stars — as he and some other select collegiate players helped the USA National Team prepare for the world championships. Jimmer said that he had fun when he learned they knew who he was and they made him feel like he belonged. He was told to "keep working hard and you're going to be here with us next year."

12 Amazing

The 2010-11 season started with high expectations. Jimmer was named a pre-season First Team All-American by the Associated Press, *Sporting News, Athlon Sports, Blue Ribbon Magazine,* former coach and TV analyst Dick Vitale, and *Sports Illustrated,* which noted: "Fredette, who pulled his name out of the NBA draft just before the deadline in May, could be the most lethal — and efficient — backcourt scorer in college hoops."

Jimmer picked up where he left off his junior year, a veritable scoring machine, averaging more than 23 points a game early in the season.

After a tough loss to UCLA, Jimmer admitted his frustration. "It's tough to handle. You don't want to lose — ever. It will be good for our team to have to go through this adversity. I don't think anybody thought we would go undefeated."

BYU bounced back and won their next ten games, including an 89-77 win over 25th ranked rival UNLV to open Mountain West Conference play. Jimmer poured in 39 points along with six rebounds and five assists.

"I was just hitting shots tonight," Jimmer said

after the game. "I saw the ball going into the basket. My teammates did a great job of screening and finding me when I was open."

Or, as the BYU fans would say, UNLV "got Jimmered!"

In early 2011, Jimmer went on a scoring tear, scoring 40 or more points in three out of four games.

He jump-started the game at BYU's arch rival Utah with 32 points in the first half — capped with a buzzer beater right past the half court line. He was pulled out with over 3 minutes left of the game. He finished with 47 points and BYU won the game by 25 points. Soon his 40-plus foot shot went viral on various video sharing networks.

"I figured I might as well try to push it and see if I could get a good shot off," Jimmer said. "It wasn't a great shot. Sometimes you get lucky like that."

By the end of January, Jimmer was the nation's leading scorer with a 27.4 average — and averaging more points on the road. On February 5, he became the Mountain West Conference's all-time leading scorer with a 29-point game against UNLV and his name was regularly mentioned as a contender for college player of the year. Jimmermania had officially arrived.

After beating San Diego State again in February, BYU was ranked third in the AP Poll, but dropped down to eighth after losing to unranked New Mexico for the second time that season.

BYU met up with New Mexico again in the conference tournament with a vengeance. Jimmer hit seven threes on his way to his career-high of 52 points. Amazingly, he only had one free throw. In that game, he set new scoring records for a single BYU game, a Mountain West Conference single-game, and for a BYU career, breaking Danny Ainge's school scoring record mark.

BYU lost in the championship game of the Mountain West Conference tournament and dropped down to tenth in the AP poll. Nevertheless, they were invited again to the NCAA Division I tournament.

Jimmer's profile was sufficiently high enough for *Sports Illustrated* to put him on their March Madness cover along with a feature about the Fredette brothers. The magazine had been following Jimmer for a year, beginning when he scored 37 points against Florida in leading the Cougars to their first NCAA Tournament victory in 2010.

Another *Sports Illustrated* article captured Jimmer's on-court flair: "It's the way he scores that's making his final season one for the hoops lexicon. Facing the opposition's best defender (or, more often, defenders), he pulls up going right or going left. He shoots off the dribble, off the wrong foot, off balance, off the glass. He finishes in traffic with a dozen deft moves, including a funky scoop shot, originating from his waist, that he can make with either hand."

The more attention he received from the media, fans, and from defenses, the better he seemed to play — especially on the road.

But even more dangerous than his offensive skills, said former Utah coach Jim Boylen, "is his swagger and confidence." Villanova coach Jay Wright added: "Players like Jimmer, it's like they have stronger mental conditioning. They can keep going with that aggressive mentality for a longer period of time."

For the second straight year, BYU advanced past the first round in the NCAA tourney, beating Wofford 74-66. Jimmer was only the third player in previous 15 NCAA tournaments with at least 30 points, 7 assists, and 4 rebounds.

In the second round against Gonzaga, it was a close game until near the middle of the second half. A quick 12-0 run turned it into a rout. The Cougars buried 14-of-28 three-pointers, including seven by Jimmer, who finished with a game-high 34 points.

The Sweet Sixteen round would be a rematch of BYU's thrilling double-overtime win over Florida in the tournament's previous year. They were tied at halftime and Jimmer was limping. In the second half, his chin was bandaged after diving to floor after giving up a steal. After eight lead changes and nine ties, BYU lost in overtime. It

Amazing

was a particularly disappointing loss for Jimmer. Despite scoring 32 points, it had been a subpar shooting night. He missed his first six shots of the game, then went 0-2 in overtime with two turnovers. He was only three for 15 behind the three point line.

"I didn't shoot the ball great," Jimmer acknowledged. "It was a credit to their defense. They did a pretty good job contesting shots. They were athletic, hedging on ball screens, doubling, switching. They did a good job but I just didn't make enough shots."

Florida coach Bill Donovan observed that Jimmer seemed to run out of gas. Jimmer didn't disagree. "Maybe a little bit at the end. We played the whole game, and I was a little bit tired. But it's not an excuse. They were ready to go, especially in that overtime. We had a chance. But they definitely had fresh legs and they were ready to go in that overtime."

Jimmer's college career was officially over but the praise and recognitions continued.

13 Drafted

Jimmer finished 2011 as the nation's leading collegiate scorer, with a 28.9 point average — and averaged more than 32 points a game in the NCAA Tournament. He ended his college career with 2,599 career points. The 1,068 points he scored his senior year were also a one-year record. His achievements were recognized by a variety of organizations.

He was named Player of the Year by the Basketball Writers Association; voted onto the Associated Press All-America team; won the 2010-11 Lowe's Senior CLASS Award, which honors the most outstanding senior student-athlete in NCAA Division I men's basketball; won the Adolph Rupp, Naismith, and Wooden Awards; was named ESPN's Best Male College Athlete of the Year at the ESPY Awards; and was named CBSSports.com's National Player of the Year.

Despite the flood of honors, there was disagreement among NBA scouts as to how Jimmer would fare as a professional. Many publications published profiles on Jimmer, some based on interviews with NBA scouts and front-office personnel.

He was generally considered offensively gifted but defensively challenged. It was said that NBA stardom was unlikely, but that he was destined to be a solid rotation player.

The consensus among the scouts and executives was that Jimmer was tentative on defense. "He appears to put in little effort so he can stay out of foul trouble and conserve energy for offense."

But BYU assistant coach Dave Rice thought the assumption was misguided, saying that a large part of Jimmer's defensive approach was by team design, not a lack of personal commitment. "A lot of that is part of our game plan. We expect so much of him on the offensive end. We can't afford to have him in foul trouble. He's a much, much better defensive player than he's given credit for."

An NBA Eastern Conference personnel director wasn't swayed. "For as sharp a shooter as he is, he's just as bad of a defender."

For his part, Jimmer considers himself "a pretty good defender. I don't think people give me as much credit as maybe I deserve on the defensive end because I do play well on the offensive end."

Although the basketball season was over, the excitement surrounding Jimmer and the upcoming NBA draft remained intense. He was more than just a big man on campus, he was a star throughout Utah and with that came the attention every celebrity experiences. So much so that Jimmer stopped going to class (per the school's request), opting to do his schoolwork online while working toward his degree.

"It was getting too disruptive," his father said. "He can't go anywhere in Provo without being recognized."

His last few months of college were a juggling act. In addition to academics, Jimmer was also laying the groundwork for a professional career, researching potential agents and ultimately signing with international sports and marketing firm Octagon to represent him. The whirlwind may have knocked a less grounded person off kilter but Jimmer's sister Lindsay said her little brother handled the extreme attention with poise.

"With media access today, people can become really well known in a short amount of time," she observed. "We always could tell that Jimmer had a special talent. We always knew he would be special to his team. But to see it blow up to this magnitude has been a surreal experience. I think back to when Jimmer was little. He was just always this unassuming, happy-go-lucky kid. He was nice and he had a cute little voice and fun-loving. When we go out with him now, so many people recognize him and they know who he is and want to be around him. It's an incredible feeling. It's exciting because it means he's reaching his goal to play in the NBA, which he is starting to realize. I'm just proud of it."

Lindsay stresses that Jimmer and the rest of the

family try to appreciate every moment. "Sometimes you take it for granted, that Jimmer's going to the NBA. You talk about it and hope for it. This doesn't happen to a lot of families. You feel excited for him and blessed to be able to be so close to it because it's such a unique experience. He's been blessed with opportunities. Hopefully he will continue to be a good influence. He's done a great job so far."

In addition, she said she was most proud of the man Jimmer had become and that he was a wonderful uncle to her kids.

With the college season over and Jimmer no longer eligible for collegiate play, he was free to professionally market himself and profit from it. In May 2011, Jimmer released a poster that touted his player of the year success.

"It's a good feeling to know you did what you had to do in college and now you are in a position where people really want to buy posters and jerseys," Jimmer noted. The poster was a way for him and his fans from across the country to celebrate the many trophies and honors.

In early summer 2011, Jimmer along with Cougar teammate Jackson Emery hosted his first summer basketball camp for kids in grades 3 through 12. Many of Jimmer's former teammates along with staff members of the athletic department participated in the camp, which provided two days worth of instruction.

"You want to give the kids the resources and the ideas of what it takes to improve," Jimmer explained.

The camp took place in between Jimmer's workouts with a series of NBA teams including the New York Knicks, Utah Jazz, Sacramento Kings, and Phoenix Suns. Although more teams wanted to have him attend their workouts, Jimmer limited his appearances. He also made it clear to Octagon that he was not going to miss the basketball camp.

"The agents work for you. You don't work for the agents," he smiled when asked during the camp. "I don't need to be over-exposed. People know who I am; they know how I play. As long as I go to these workouts and show well, it'll be okay."

Despite his phenomenal senior year at BYU, some pro scouts still doubted Jimmer was suited to point guard and others thought he wouldn't cut it as a shooting guard, either. "It was something I wanted to focus on in these workouts," he admitted. "I had a perception and it's something I had to go out and prove. People had to see it in order to believe it."

Through it all, Jimmer kept his confidence. "It's just going out there and believing in yourself ... knowing that you've put in the time, knowing that you've worked really hard to get here and now it's time for it to pay off."

When asked to describe his game, Jimmer compared himself to NBA player Deron Williams. "He's about my size. He's got a great crossover and step back. I watched him play in Utah, so I tried to emulate his game. He's obviously a very good point guard. I'm [also] somewhat a Steve Nash type. I can get my shot off quickly, especially in the lane, shooting all those different shots in my arsenal. I'm not at their level yet, but some of that stuff is in my game."

But Jimmer's hoops hero was John Stockton, "because the Jazz was my favorite team, even though they got beat by Michael Jordan every year. I've tried to model my game after him, and if I ever get to that level, I'd like to be like him." But his personal heroes were his parents: "They've been there for me whatever I've been doing. They've been big role models and without them I wouldn't be where I am."

If there was another thing Jimmer was clear on, it was priorities, which included being there for friends. As popular as he was and with all the great things that were happening to him, he still took the time to check in on his friends. He would seek out friend's parents in the stands to visit with or he'd call up his friend's families to congratulate them on *their* endeavors.

His father would tell him: "You can be the best basketball player in the world, but if you're not a nice person, it wouldn't mean anything."

As one example, when leaving an arena at a

Drafted

high school tournament, Jimmer stopped to help a man move some heavy jugs of water; when done he was asked: "Hey, aren't you the guy that just scored 36?"

After visiting a former AAU teammate in a hospital and invited him to attend the NBA draft, his friend's father said that Jimmer was "just an incredible young man who puts himself behind everybody."

Chris Carson, another old AAU teammate, said: "The thing that everyone can learn from Jimmer is the old saying, that good things happen to good people, is true. I never heard Jimmer say a bad thing about anybody. Playing AAU, a system that has ruined some good basketball players by pumping up their egos and introducing them to the wrong people, Jimmer always remained the same kid. Always remained respectful. He never pretended to be too good for anyone."

June 23, 2011, would be all about Jimmer as a new chapter in his life was about to start.

Four and a half years after signing it, Jimmer was about to take another big step toward fulfilling his contract with T.J.and himself to become a professional NBA basketball player. And his entire family planned to be part of his special night.

"It will be a unique thing and a special moment for Jimmer," his sister said. "We want to support him and celebrate with him, hopefully, afterwards. It will be an exciting moment. Something we'll remember for a long time. We want to be able to experience it as a family."

She admitted she was hoping her brother would be drafted by the Utah Jazz. "For my own interests, I'd like to see him with the Jazz because I would be able to see him more often and he'd be close. It would be a real fun thing for me."

T.J. had other ideas. "We want him to go to the Knicks. That's our team."

Personal interests aside, the whole family wanted to see him go somewhere that was a good situation for him — where he would have the opportunity to improve his skills by playing and learning from other players. They wanted him to get a team where the coach and front office personnel all valued him.

There was little doubt he would be a first round pick but there was no clear consensus among sports writers as to how high he would go. The Milwaukee Bucks ended the suspense when they drafted Jimmer tenth. But his selection was strategic: the Bucks were using Jimmer as trade bait for a three-team deal between Milwaukee, the Charlotte Hornets, and Sacramento. Within hours of being the No. 10 pick in the draft, Jimmer was a Sacramento King. To get Jimmer and an experienced NBA player, they had traded a player and given up the No. 7 pick in the draft.

His fans in New York were ecstatic, proudly noting that Jimmer became just the fourth player from a Section II high school selected in the first round of the NBA draft, after Sam Perkins, Pat Riley, and Barry Kramer.

Don Landrio, who coached at Gloversville, commented on Jimmer's growth as a person. "What he has carried on right through his college career is his role model stature. He certainly is a player who you would want your child to be like. That is something his parents should be proud of."

His former AAU teammate Kevin Kucel said it was no surprise that Jimmer was a top ten draft pick. "I feel there is no way he is not going to succeed. Every time we were in practice, every drill we did, everything was a competition. I am just really excited for him. He is really fun to watch."

Two days after the draft, Jimmer flew to Sacramento and was met by several hundred fans crowding around the baggage claim area welcoming him to their city. Jimmer took the attention in stride and took time to sign autographs. Although some local sports writers and bloggers were taking a wait and see attitude as to whether Jimmer would be a boom or a bust, the fans had clearly embraced Jimmermania.

Although he was only in Sacramento for two days, Jimmer took time to visit his new LDS congregation. At the gathering, Jimmer answered some basketball related questions and asserted plans to be active in the church and make the time to speak at Sacramento-area church youth group meetings.

One person who attended the get-together told a local newspaper: "A lot of people who may have gone to a game or two are now buying season tickets."

But it would be a while before the King faithful would get to see their newest acquisition in action. Jimmer and the rest of the NBA players had to put their professional life on hold as the owners initiated a lockout after failing to reach a new contract with the players' union. With both sides digging in, many worried the entire 2011-12 season might be lost.

14 Lockout

On July 1, 2011, team owners locked out the players, unable to agree on the division of revenues and other changes owners wanted in a new collective bargaining agreement; specifically, making it more difficult for star players to leave smaller market teams. The situation left many players in limbo. Some considered playing in Europe, but not knowing how long the lockout would last made committing to a foreign team risky. Some players approached it as an extended vacation, others used the time to work on their games and stay sharp so they'd be ready whenever the lockout ended.

Jimmer tried to balance his personal life with his eagerness to stay prepared for his professional debut — whenever that would be. Shortly after his first trip to Sacramento, Jimmer was invited to take part in a celebrity golf tournament in Lake Tahoe. The participants included Michael Jordan, Charles Barkley, and former NFL quarterback Trent Green.

Back home in Glens Falls, Jimmer spent time with friends, and worked with kids at the Super

Hooper Basketball Camp run by Coach Hammel, before flying back to Utah to start training for his rookie season.

The lockout meant that all NBA arenas and training facilities were off limits to players as long as the labor dispute continued. So Jimmer went to Provo, and worked out on his own and with other players.

"There's a few ex-NBA and current NBA players out there in that Utah area," his father Al told a reporter. "Jimmer needs to be in great shape so he works real hard. He does a lot of sprints for running. He doesn't do any distance, but very high-end sprints. Then he does jumping drills, rebounding, works on agility, practices defensive slides, dribbling drills and shooting. He really covers them all. He's really working hard trying to stay in top condition. That's important, especially if you're going to be a running team, which I think they will be."

Al also noted that because of the lockout, Jimmer hadn't been able to sign his contract with the Kings, which was another reason he was in Utah and not California.

"There's no sense going to Sacramento and renting a place for the next three or four months if you're not going to be using it," Al explained. "He's got some endorsements and things, but he's not making tons of money, so he's got to be careful about his money. For now he's in Provo. A guy

Lockout

out there is letting him stay in his house. Plus, he's got a place to work out. So he'll be in Utah until we hear that things might start getting close to a settlement. He's just going to keep training hard. That's a big part of his day."

But it wasn't always easy, Jimmer admitted. "You know, it's a grind. You've got to go out and practice. I always work out two times a day. In the morning I will go do my lifting and my explosive drills and conditioning. Then in the afternoons I will do all my basketball skill work. It's a good contrast. The biggest part about it is normally the off-season would be over now, but you need to continue to work as if it's the off-season, to keep yourself motivated and get better even though you're not playing or practicing."

Originally, the Kings were scheduled to open at home on November 2 against the Houston Rockets. But as the lockout lingered, the league eventually cancelled all the November games. It was an especially frustrating time for incoming rookies.

"You want to get your career started, to be in the NBA and fulfill your dream, but it's just on hold right now. I hope that both sides come to an agreement fairly soon and I hope that it's a good deal for both sides. Hopefully, they will come to an agreement soon ... and we can start playing basketball again."

Just because he couldn't yet play for the Kings

didn't mean Jimmer couldn't find a way to play. He would make his professional debut in an exhibition game held in Utah in September. The event was called *Jimmer's All-Stars Presented by Zions Bank* and included other 2011 draftees.

In a statement released to the media in August, Jimmer said: "I'm really looking forward to making my debut as a professional in front of the fans who have so passionately supported me during my time at BYU. This will be a fun opportunity to bring some other NBA draftees to Utah for the chance to play competitive basketball."

But the biggest news Jimmer shared in August was of a more personal nature. He announced his engagement to longtime girlfriend and BYU cheerleader Whitney Wonnacott on Twitter.

"I'm officially engaged everyone. She said yes and she was completely surprised! It was perfect!!"

Jimmer also revealed the couple planned to get married in 2012 in the Denver LDS Temple. "She will graduate in April and then go back to Denver to start getting everything ready for the wedding. She will come and visit whenever she can. So that's how we're going to have to do it until June 1." (They were married the following year as planned.)

In September, over 11,000 fans attended his charity game in Provo. Eight first-round draft picks and four second-rounders competed in the high-scoring game — and marked a professional

Lockout

debut for some as they were paid a nice appearance fee. And in November, Jimmer and other professionals played in the Pro Players Charity Classic in Salt Lake City and at the Goon Squad Classic in Davis, California.

"It was great to talk to them and get to know what to expect when we get into the season," he said about his opportunity to play with the NBA stars.

15 Sacramento's New King

On November 26, 2011, the NBA owners and players' union announced a new labor agreement, ending the nearly five month lockout. The deal called for a 66 game season in 2011-12, scheduled to begin on Christmas Day.

On December 9, the Kings announced they signed his contract and Jimmer tweeted "I'm finally an NBA basketball player now!" Per the team's policy, the terms of the deal were not disclosed. The NBA has defined maximum salaries for first round picks based on their draft position (to prevent rookies from holding out for salaries higher that experienced veterans). Jimmer's contract for two years is worth around $4 million.

The King's first preseason game, and Jimmer's NBA debut, took place December 17 against the Golden State Warriors. Although Sacramento lost, Jimmer picked up where he left off at BYU, scoring 21 points and going 4 for 6 from three-point range, and ending with four assists.

Paul Westphal, his first NBA coach, gave the

rookie encouraging remarks: "He's a basketball player. He understands what he's doing and why and I thought he did a good job. They tried to post him up with a bigger guy and he did a really nice job two or three times."

Westphal also complimented Jimmer's defense. "I thought it was everything you would hope for with a player who is coming into the league for his first game who is not known as a defensive player. He held his own just fine. Offensively, he looked very comfortable and made good decisions."

Warriors coach Mark Jackson also thought Jimmer played well. "It was very good to see him, live and in person. He's tough, hard-nosed, gritty and obviously shot the lights out. Very impressive, I thought at times we allowed him to get us on our heels ... he played very well."

When asked what it was like playing in the NBA, he smiled. "It's still basketball. It's a little different, the guys are bigger, a little bit more athletic and guys can really shoot the ball and score. It's pretty much what I thought, but you don't know what is going to happen until you go through it so it was a good learning experience. I went out there and competed, got hands in shooters' faces and tried to force tough shots. I got a steal or two and I thought I did well."

After their opening game win over the Los Angeles Lakers, the Kings — and Jimmer — started the regular season poorly. In his first few weeks, he was shooting only 33 percent and averaging around 7 points. After a two win and five loss start to the season, the Kings coach was fired and the assistant Keith Smart was signed as the new head coach.

Similar to his beginnings as a freshman in high school and in college, his rookie campaign started slowly but with some good highlights.

Due to a teammate's injury, Jimmer was able to start a few games and during one stretch of four straight double-digit scoring games, he averaged 14.2 points per game and hit 15-of-25 from beyond the arc. On January 21, he set his early NBA career-highs against the Memphis Grizzlies with 20 points, 6 assists, and 7 free throws. But after his success, he sat out two games due to a coaching decision.

Jimmer said that consistency is a challenge for rookies a lot of times, and that was what he was working on.

"When I get into the game, I just play as hard as I can — the shots will fall," he said. "I just go out there and do whatever it is that the coach wants me to do, and whatever it is that's best to help the team win that night."

He came back strong — against the Timberwolves, he led a furious comeback attempt with three consecutive triples, two assists, and 13 points all in the fourth quarter.

Nearly two months into the season, Jimmer

ranked second in three-pointers, seventh in scoring, and ninth in assists among all the rookies.

As the season progressed, he became more comfortable and averaged 11 points per game for his last six games. The Kings finished in last place for their Pacific Division and didn't make the playoffs. "I don't know if I've ever had a losing season," Jimmer said.

Jimmer finished the abbreviated season with 462 points, 78 three pointers, and 108 assists. Per minute played for the Kings, he was fifth in points and fourth for assists and shot an above average 36 percent for threes.

Now that he's reached his goal of the NBA, Jimmer continues to be a role model — and inspiration — for countless kids. His advice, especially to those diamonds in the rough like he was as a chubby grade schooler, is to keep at it:

"I would tell them to dream big. If you work as hard as you can and really believe in yourself, then you can accomplish anything. It doesn't matter where you are from or what high school you went to, you can still accomplish your dreams. I'm from a small high school in upstate New York and not many people knew about me, but I had a dream, went out and worked as hard as I could for it and accomplished it."

What he accomplishes next nobody knows, but it sure will be fun to watch.

Selected References

Allen J. Fredette to the rescue. *Times Union.* January 6, 2007.
Allen J. Rocks root for Fredette. *Times Union.* March 25, 2011.
Anderson K. A Real Jimmer Dandy. *Sports Illustrated.* January 31, 2011.
Blow D. Q&A with Jimmer Fredette. *The Post-Star.* March 21, 2007.
Call J. BYU basketball: Big sis played big hand in Jimmer Fredette's development. *Deseret News.* June 6, 2011.
Call J. BYU basketball: Jimmer Fredette, brother to be profiled in Sports Illustrated. *Deseret News.* January 27, 2011.
Connelly C. Bond of Brothers [Video]. *ESPN.* February 5, 2011.
Dravis, S. Glens Falls squeaks by determined Hudson Falls. *The Post-Star.* February 21, 2005.
Dravis, S. Sophomores lead Glens Falls past Saratoga. *The Post-Star.* December 5, 2004.
Drew J. BYU basketball: Fredette's 49 helps Cougars crush Arizona. *The Salt Lake Tribune.* December 28, 2009.
Ellis J. All Hail King Jimmer. *The Leader Herald.* June 26, 2011.
Fagan K. Dribble to the light. *The Post-Star.* February 19, 2008.
Fagan K. Jimmer Fredette's unlikely path to becoming a star. *The Philadelphia Inquirer.* March 15, 2011.
Franchuk J. A look back: Jimmer finds way to BYU with a big assist from a Syracuse coach. *Daily Herald.* December 5, 2010.
Franchuk J. Jimmer enjoys "camping" for the first time in Utah. *Daily Herald.* June 5, 2011.
Franchuk J. Jimmer to host 2 NBA rookie all-star games in Utah. *Daily Herald.* August 23, 2011.
Fredette scores 46 in G.F. blowout. *The Post-Star.* February 10, 2007.
Garcia M. Jimmer Fredette drops 47; No. 10 Brigham Young rolls Utah. *USA Today.* January 11, 2011.
Garza J. Mormon fans have faith in Kings draft pick Jimmer Fredette. *The Sacramento Bee.* July 6, 2011.
Hansen T. Talkin' with Trav: Q&A with Jimmer Fredette. *Deseret News.* November 1, 2011.
Iorizzo P. Fredette's will to win began early. *Times Union.* December 5, 2010.
Jimmer's Uncle Lee Breaks Down His Workouts [Video]. *Youtube.* June 9, 2011.
Jones D. Talor Battle knew Jimmer Fredette was a player when they were on same AAU team. *The Patriot-News.* January 28, 2011.
Kramers A. How Sacramento's Jimmer Fredette Got His Groove Back. *Blogcritics.org.* February 8, 2012.
Layden T. With a crowd behind him, Fredette hoping to take BYU to new heights. *Sports Illustrated.* March 18, 2009.

Beyond the Arc

Lewis M. A connection on any field. *The Post-Star.* October 3, 2005.

Lloyd J. Jimmer, Burks show stuff in SLC charity game. *Daily Herald.* november 8, 2011.

Marshall K. Different players, same record. *The Post-Star.* December 24, 2006.

Martinez K. BYU basketball: Jimmer Fredette injured in workout with Knicks, will announce plans on Saturday. *Examiner*.com. May 7, 2010.

McCord K. TJ Fredette talks about growing up with Jimmer. *KSL.* January 26, 2011.

McManus T. Glens Falls rises to the finals. *The Post-Star.* March 18, 2007.

McMurphy, B. Jimmer Fredette Takes No Prisoners. *Aol News.* March 19, 2010.

Medved E. *Jimmer Fredette, King of our area courts, is now truly a King! Albany Times Union.* June 24, 2011.

Moore J. Jimmer isn't Tebow, but they are really close. *KSL.* March 20, 2011.

Orr C. NBA Draft 2011: Jimmer Fredette makes good on his deal as the 10th pick. *The Star-Ledger.* June 24, 2011.

Ortiz M. Growing Up with Jimmer Fredette: Everything You Didn't Know. *Bleacher Report.* March 12, 2011.

Orzechowski B. It just wasn't meant to be. *The Post-Star.* March 2, 2005.

Orzechowski B. Striving for perfection. *The Post-Star.* January 7, 2005.

Peekskill breathes sigh, edges Glens Falls. *Times Warner Cable Sports.* March 18, 2007.

Post P. NBA: Jimmer to stay in USA. *The Saratogian.* August 9, 2011.

Robinson D. Jimmer Fredette, BYU guard, returns to play in his New York home town. *Deseret News.* December 8, 2010.

SI.com's preseason All-Americas. *Sports Illustrated.* November 8, 2010.

Santiago J. Kings at Warriors: Jimmer shows well in preseason opener. *Cowbell Kingdom.* December 17, 2011.

Springstead W. A full-fledged Cougar. *The Post-Star.* November 20, 2007.

Springstead W. Catch a rising star: Glens Falls' Jimmer Fredette developing into complete player. *The Post-Star.* December, 24, 2005.

Springstead W. Fredette headed west. *The Post-Star.* September 14, 2006.

Springstead W. Indians claim Foothills. *The Post-Star.* February 15, 2006.

Springstead W. Is this the year? *The Post-Star.* March 16, 2007.

Springstead W. Peekskill retains title by downing Glens Falls. *The Post-Star.* March 19, 2007.

TJ Fredette: Jimmers Brother Finds His Rhythm In Rap. *Lost Lettermen.* February 1, 2011.

Thamel P. N.B.A. Scouting Report on Fredette: Good but Not Great. *The New York Times.* March 23, 2011.

Thamel P. Where The Show Started. *The New York Times.* February 26, 2011.

Thompson M. Jimmer visits his old elementary school for one last time. *The Post-Star.* June 18, 2011.

Tingley K. BYU says Jimmer is too cool for school. *The Post-Star.* April 8, 2011.

Tobey P. Fredette was also pretty talented in football. *The Post-Star.* December 6, 2010.

Tobey P. Glens Falls' Fredette, Wilhelm lead AAU team at nationals. *The Post-Star.* August 3, 2006.

Zeigler M. The story behind the Jimmer. *San Diego Union-Tribune.* February 24, 2011.

Acknowledgements

I gratefully acknowledge teammate Chris Carson, Coach Tony Hammel, and Coach Eric Medved for their feedback and information and the reviewers for their excellent critiques of various drafts: Ellen Caffry, Kyle Rapoza, Sarah E. Reed, Jorem Krieg, Diane Krieg, Desiree Reynolds, Heather Reed, and Payton Reed. This book wouldn't exist without the awesome writing by the co-author Kathy Tracy. I owe thanks most of all, though, to my family — Heather, Austin, Avery, Adrion, Payton, Parker, Kaden, Landon, and Sarah — for being curious, excited, and patient while they read or listened to the stories again and again.

As I researched, the more I learned that Jimmer's and his family's stories were inspiring for us. As we watched him play on TV and in person, I saw that his joy and skills reminded me of my childhood teammates and playground friends. I planned and co-authored this book for my eight children, who I love to dribble and shoot with, other youth readers, and for his many fans — may they be influenced to challenge themselves, set goals, work hard, remain respectful, and, as his teammate told me, learn that in life it is not always about what you do, but the way in which you do it.

— *Jeremy C. Reed*

Also from the publisher

The book *Beginning Boy Scouts* (ISBN 978-1-937516-01-7), a practical guide to the Boy Scouts of America, quickly answers numerous common questions and provides instruction and advice for concerned and desperate parents and leaders — to help know "what is first?" and how to get started, preparing for outdoor activities and summer camp, uniforms, leadership and the Patrol method, earning awards and badges, Eagle planning, how to participate, and a lot more. See the book's webpage at *http://www.reedmedia.net/books/beginning-boy-scouts/* for reviews.

www.ingramcontent.com/pod-product-compliance
Lightning Source LLC
Chambersburg PA
CBHW071313040426
42444CB00009B/1998